A CAREER AS A
POLICE
OFFICER

STEPHANIE WATSON

JAN - - 2011

ROSEN
PUBLISHING
NEW YORK

To all the brave men and women
who put their lives on the line to protect us every day

Published in 2011 by The Rosen Publishing Group, Inc.
29 East 21st Street, New York, NY 10010

Library of Congress Cataloging-in-Publication Data

Watson, Stephanie, 1969–
A career as a police officer / Stephanie Watson.—1st ed.
    p. cm.—(Essential careers)
Includes bibliographical references and index.
ISBN 978-1-4358-9469-3 (library binding)
1. Police—Vocational guidance—United States—Juvenile literature. 2. Law enforcement—Vocational guidance—United States—Juvenile literature. I. Title.
HV7922.W38 2011
363.2023'73—dc22

2009040001

Manufactured in the United States of America

CPSIA Compliance Information: Batch #S10YA: For further information, contact Rosen Publishing, New York, New York, at 1-800-237-9932.

contents

INTRO

Police officers often patrol neighborhoods looking for crime suspects. This Fairfax County, Virginia, police officer watches for signs of suspicious activity near a hardware store where a murder was committed.

DUCTION

A disturbed man steals a military tank from a National Guard Armory in southern California. San Diego police give chase as the tank driver barrels over cars and threatens motorists and pedestrians on a residential street. The crazed driver heads onto the freeway—right into oncoming traffic. When the tank stops for a moment, police officers bravely jump onto it and force the hatch open, ending the ordeal.

Undercover police officers in Washington State enroll at three area high schools. They've heard that an illegal drug and gun operation may be running out of the schools. The officers pose as students and pretend they want to buy drugs and guns. Students who have been operating the drug and gun ring fall for the scheme, and the undercover officers arrest them.

On March 30, 1981, President Ronald Reagan stops to wave to crowds outside of a Hilton Hotel in Washington, D.C. A disturbed man named John Hinckley Jr. shoots at him from the crowd. Secret Service agent Timothy McCarthy jumps between the president and his attacker. The president is wounded, but not critically. McCarthy is shot in the chest, but he survives.

A killer terrorizes women in Seattle, Washington. The police have a short list of suspects, but they don't have enough proof to arrest or charge anyone. The case goes cold. A decade later, forensic investigators reopen the case using bits of DNA taken from the crime scenes. They find a match. The killer is arrested and charged with the crimes.

A police car zooms down a city street. Officers often have to patrol at night, which can be dangerous. Research shows that criminals are more likely to use a gun or other weapon at night than during the day.

These examples illustrate just how important law enforcement officers are to public safety. Every day, they put their own lives in danger to protect the lives of others. They work to keep communities, homes, businesses, schools, and just about every other place safe. Officers do everything from preventing and solving crimes to directing traffic and keeping order at public events.

Law enforcement is a recession-proof career. Why? Because crime doesn't go away when the economy takes a downturn. In fact, corporate layoffs and shrinking paychecks can lead to a spike in crime as people become angry and desperate for money. That means there is always plenty of work for police and other law enforcement officers.

Police departments are not completely safe from budget cuts, however. In one survey conducted by the Police Executive Research Forum during an economic slump, 63 percent of the departments said they were planning to cut funding. Less funding means less money for officer salaries. Sometimes police departments that don't have enough money to fund their efforts will put an end to a job when the officer who holds it retires or chooses to leave. In some cases, they may even cut jobs. On the whole, the law enforcement field still has plenty of opportunities for talented and hard-working people.

When exploring career options, students should think carefully about what they want in a job. For anyone who loves excitement, wants a steady job with good benefits and security, and is willing to take risks, law enforcement might be the perfect career choice.

chapter 1

HAVING A CAREER AS A POLICE OFFICER

The main job of a police officer is enforcing laws to protect people and their property. That role remains pretty much the same for any job in this profession, from a patrol officer, to a detective, to an agent with the Federal Bureau of Investigation (FBI).

The exact responsibilities can be different, based on the type of position an officer holds. A police officer may respond to calls about crimes being committed, or he or she may patrol an area to prevent crimes from occurring. The officer might catch a person who is in the middle of committing a crime or—in the example of a detective—investigate a case until the criminal is found and arrested.

A big part of the job of a police officer involves working at a desk, filling out paperwork. Officers have to keep careful records of their investigations. Those records may be used in court to provide the evidence needed to put a suspect behind bars. Sometimes police officers may have to testify in court. They will sit on the witness stand and tell the judge and jury what happened during a robbery, murder, or other case.

Officers, whether they are on patrol or working at a desk, have a great deal of authority. People are expected to follow any directions an officer gives them. Law enforcement

PROFILE OF AN OFFICER

Kevin Murtagh majored in art and design while he was in college. He started his career in photojournalism (taking the photographs that appear next to stories in the newspapers). After ten years, he decided to change jobs. Having seen his father and uncle work on the police force, Murtagh eventually decided he wanted to follow in their footsteps. He has been with the Police Department of South Plainfield, New Jersey, for about twenty years. In that time, he has had many responsibilities.

During his five years on patrol, Murtagh answered calls for incidents ranging from burglaries to assaults. Sometimes he'd have to go out at 1:30 AM to break up fights. Murtagh also spent time on a narcotics task force. He and his fellow officers went undercover, pretending they were landscape workers. They drove into areas where they knew drugs were being sold. "I would pull up next to a drug dealer and try to buy," he says. "We'd go back another night to try to get the second deal. Then we'd get a warrant and lock them [the drug dealers] up."

As a detective, Murtagh investigated burglaries, murders and other types of deaths, bad checks, and crimes related to illegal drugs. He collected evidence at crime scenes, interviewed witnesses, and did everything he could to solve cases. Today, he is a lieutenant. Murtagh is looking forward to retiring in five years after twenty-five years on the police force.

officers of all kinds usually wear uniforms and badges to show their positions. Some states require their officers to wear protective body armor, also called bulletproof vests. Officers carry a gun and other special equipment, such as handcuffs, a baton, or a Taser, that can help them catch criminals.

Main Responsibilities of a Police Officer

A police officer's job varies from day to day and from department to department. As officers gain more experience, their roles also can change. The following are just a few of the tasks that the members of a police department might perform on an average day:

Patrol neighborhoods. Officers travel through their beat, the area they are assigned to patrol by car, motorcycle, bicycle, or on foot. Patrolling gives local law enforcement officers a chance to get to know the

Patrolling on a bicycle can allow police officers to easily navigate crowded city streets. Bicycling also gives officers the chance to get to know community residents.

people who live in their area, and it helps local residents learn to trust the officers. Becoming familiar with a community can help the police spot suspicious activity when it does occur. Officers patrol alone or with partners. While on patrol, they may have to pursue and arrest people who are breaking the law.

Arrest criminals. Often, dispatchers will call officers to the scene of a bank robbery, burglary, assault, or other crime. The officers may have to pursue suspects on foot or by car, and they may have to use a gun, or other type of weapon, or force to catch them. Once suspects have been caught and arrested, the officer frisks them to make sure they are not carrying any weapons or drugs. The officer reads them their legal rights (called Miranda rights, which begin with the words, "You have the right to remain silent") and transports them to a facility where they are booked for the crime.

Investigate crimes. To investigate a crime, police officers must

Part of a law enforcement officer's job may involve collecting evidence at the scene of a crime. This crime specialist is looking for clues to help solve a case.

visit the crime scene, interview witnesses, and collect the evidence (material objects such as fingerprints and hair) that they need to solve the case.

Write reports. Police officers have to keep very detailed reports of the crimes they investigate. They may have to present these reports as evidence during a trial.

Enforce traffic laws. Police officers patrol highways and local roads to catch people who violate traffic laws by speeding or running traffic lights. They give out traffic tickets and citations to motorists who break the law, including those who commit vehicle violations and who are suspected of driving while under the influence of alcohol or drugs. Police officers also direct traffic when there is a car accident, a broken traffic light, or a major event like a concert or demonstration. They might also have to reroute traffic when there is an emergency, such as a flood, downed power line, or other safety hazard. A police officer arriving at the scene of a car accident may have to administer first aid to an injured person until an ambulance arrives.

Some of the other duties a police officer might have to perform include the following:

- Check a warehouse or office building at night to make sure it is secure.

One job responsibility of an officer might be to keep the peace at public demonstrations. Police officers are seen here trying to keep protestors at an antiwar rally under control.

- Settle a dispute between a husband and wife (domestic dispute).
- Deliver a baby.
- Report potholes, broken traffic lights, or other potentially dangerous road conditions.

Since the terrorist attacks of September 11, 2001, security has increased at the nation's airports. This police officer conducts a passenger check at Logan International Airport in Boston, Massachusetts.

- Search for a missing person.
- Recover stolen property.
- Conduct a criminal background check.
- Watch a person or location (conduct surveillance) for suspicious or unlawful activity.

- Assist emergency medical crews or stranded motorists.
- Evacuate people from dangerous situations.
- Issue parking tickets.
- Maintain his or her patrol car and weapons.

Police officers deal with the daily concerns of people in the community, encourage crime prevention efforts, and preserve the peace.

WHAT LAW ENFORCEMENT OFFICERS DO FROM DAY TO DAY

The following are some of the positions in law enforcement and some of the usual duties an officer might expect to have during a typical day:

Detective. A murder has been committed. A detective is assigned to the case. First, the detective visits the crime scene to gather evidence. Collecting evidence could involve dusting glasses for fingerprints, plucking a few stray hairs off the carpet for DNA analysis, taking pictures of the crime scene, and collecting bullet fragments from the victim.

Sheriffs are responsible for prisoners held in their county. Sometimes, prisoners must be supervised while on work detail, which can include picking up trash as part of a group that labors outside the prison.

Then the detective interviews a witness who was at the scene shortly after the crime was committed, as well as a few neighbors who heard the shot. All the evidence that is collected goes back to the forensics lab for analysis. The fingerprints and DNA samples are compared to computer data of samples taken from people who have committed crimes. After enough evidence has been collected, the detective prepares a report and submits it to his or her superior officer. If the detective has done his or her job correctly, a suspect will be arrested and the case will be closed. But if there is not enough evidence, a case may remain open for many years.

Sheriff. The local sheriff is the warden of the county jail. When suspects are arrested, the sheriff is responsible for processing them and keeping them in custody. The sheriff also makes sure that the jail runs properly and all the prisoners are cared for appropriately.

Highway patrol officer. Late at night, the highway patrol officer is positioned on the side of a major highway. The officer looks for cars that are being driven unusually (such as those that weave from side to side) or too fast. When the driver of a car exceeds the speed limit, the officer signals for the driver to pull over. He or she collects the driver's license and car registration card and has the driver's background checked

Transit authority police officers patrol subways to ensure that passengers stay safe. The New York City subways are some of the busiest in the nation, with more than a billion passengers riding each year.

for any history of violations or arrest warrants. Then the officer issues the driver a traffic ticket.

Transit authority officer. The transit authority officer is assigned to patrol the subway in a big city. During a shift,

the officer walks through subway stations, watching for illegal activity. He or she may investigate a suspicious package, clear the station of panhandlers, or catch someone who has stolen a subway rider's wallet or purse.

Drug Enforcement Administration (DEA) agent. There is evidence that a drug ring is working out of a house in a quiet suburban neighborhood. DEA agents go undercover. They pose as homeowners in the neighborhood and closely monitor everyone who goes into or out of the house in question. After they have gathered enough evidence to prove that the homeowners are involved in illegal drug activity, they raid the house and arrest everyone inside.

K-9 officer. The K-9 officer's dog is his or her partner and constant companion on the job, whether it's at an airport,

PROFILE OF A CANADIAN OFFICER

When Jennifer McFeggan was growing up in Ontario, Canada, a local safety officer visited her elementary school. Right away, she knew exactly what she wanted to do for a living. "He stood for all things good and for keeping all of us safe," she recalls. "I was hooked!"

At the time, McFeggan didn't know of any female police officers where she lived, but she saw the male-dominated profession as a challenge. "As a woman in this field, you do have to prove yourself more than a guy would," she says. "When [I was] at the Canadian Police College, there were twenty-five guys and me. The teacher kept calling us 'men' and got very upset with me when I corrected him."

After graduating from college, McFeggan got a job working in general patrol for the Hamilton Police Service. She also worked in forensics and on the riot squad, and she helped stop illegal drug activity. McFeggan has seen a lot during her career, including a baby that was born in a car on the way to the hospital. She also has saved many lives.

Today, McFeggan is a police constable. She has had many accomplishments during her eighteen years with the Hamilton Police Service. "A few years ago, my former teacher asked me to speak at my high school. It really made me reflect on my career, and I was very proud of policing," she says.

seaport, or at the U.S. border shared with Mexico or Canada. At an airport, for example, they work together as a team. When the officer hears that a suitcase has just arrived on a flight from Honduras and it might contain illegal drugs, the officer walks his or her dog around the baggage claim. The dog sniffs the bags coming off the carousel until it stops at one that smells suspicious. The officer opens the suitcase, finds the drugs, and arrests the owner.

These job responsibilities differ based on the department, location, and position within the department. To find out exactly what one of these positions involves, it can be helpful to visit a local law enforcement office and meet the officers working in that particular job.

chapter 2

GETTING THAT FIRST JOB AS A POLICE OFFICER

Becoming a police officer is far more complicated than just walking into the local police station, filling out a job application, and getting the job. Getting hired as a police officer requires skill, training, and the successful completion of a long application process. People who are interested in pursuing a career in law enforcement can start their training as early as high school.

HIGH SCHOOL AND COLLEGE COURSES

High schools usually don't have police officer programs, but many high school classes offer good preparation for the field. Physical education (PE), Spanish or another foreign language, English, and math are all useful skills for this career path. A few high schools, such as Meade High School at Fort Meade in Maryland, offer a four-year program in domestic security to help students prepare for careers in homeland security. Besides the standard high school classes, students in such programs can take courses on topics that include nuclear arms, cyber crimes, and domestic militias. Other high schools, such as Murrieta High School in Murrieta, California, offer classes in forensic science and law enforcement. These courses provide students with entry-level skills in crime scene photography, evidence collection, fingerprinting, analysis of tool patterns, theories of crime and punishment, ethical practices, search and seizure, gang awareness, patrol tactics, and legal and moral issues.

Many junior colleges, colleges, and universities offer degrees in law enforcement. A background in political science, computer science, law, psychology, sociology, or criminal justice also can be a plus in this field. Majoring in a foreign language, particularly Spanish, is helpful, especially for officers working in cities where there are large populations of non-English-speaking residents. Participating in the Reserve Officers' Training Corps (ROTC) or another military program can teach the skills necessary for the job,

Starting in high school, students can learn many of the skills needed for a law enforcement career. This forensics class is learning how to investigate a murder and arson scene.

including the use of firearms. Military veterans are given an advantage over other applicants when they apply for police positions.

PERSONAL QUALIFICATIONS

Applicants for a job as a police officer must be U.S. citizens. They usually have to be at least twenty-one years old. However, some police departments hire eighteen-year-olds as cadets or interns and then train them in basic police skills for a couple of years. Once they turn twenty-one, the cadets or interns may be considered for a position in the regular police force. (Still, some states and counties will allow trainees to become officers at a younger age.)

Because it is a police officer's job to uphold the law, applicants cannot have had any felony convictions. (Background

Police departments will usually announce when they are holding police exams. Sometimes, however, they will allow people to fill out applications at a job fair like this one in New York City.

checks will confirm this, so it is important to be truthful on applications and in interviews.) People who have domestic violence convictions or have used drugs recently cannot become law enforcement officers. They also must never have been fired from a job for poor behavior or have received a dishonorable discharge from the U.S. military. Young people with goals of becoming a police officer should have a good driving history and manage their money wisely. Prospective employers will look closely at candidates' financial backgrounds to ensure that their applicants are responsible citizens.

The best law enforcement officers are honest, trustworthy, intelligent, and have good leadership abilities and excellent judgment. They are emotionally stable—they are able to control their anger and emotions in even the most dangerous situations. Officers also need to be healthy and strong enough to handle the tough physical demands of the job, such as chasing after criminals. People who meet these requirements and are up to the challenges of being a police officer can start looking for open positions in a police department in their region.

TESTING

When a police force is hiring, it will post an announcement that it is holding a police exam. People who are interested in a job can fill out an application, which includes a list of questions about their education, past employment experience, and other personal information. If they meet the basic qualifications for the police department, they will be invited to take the written exam—the first step in the police application process.

Applicants must pass the written exam before they can even be considered for a job. The written exam ensures that applicants are able to understand materials, such as laws

The police officer exam tests applicants' mental and physical skills. Part of the physical test may involve dragging a heavy dummy to prove that you're strong enough for the job.

and handbooks, and communicate effectively. It also tells whether or not applicants can respond appropriately to the types of situations they would encounter while on the police force. The higher an applicant's score, the faster that person is considered for an open position. Candidates who fail the written test the first time may be allowed to take it again at a later time.

Most tests include multiple-choice questions, but a few require applicants to answer written questions about a scene they watch in a video, or write an original passage that shows their reasoning and writing skills. Questions usually include the following: reading comprehension (to see how well the applicant understands information presented in a passage and makes decisions based on that information), basic math (addition, subtraction, multiplication, and division), memory, grammar and spelling, and map reading.

Candidates who pass the written test will also need to take a physical ability test to make sure they can handle the physical demands of the job. This test measures speed, strength, and agility. It may involve challenges like running, doing sit-ups and push-ups, and completing obstacle courses. A standard fitness test may involve the following tasks:

- Run up and down a flight of stairs.
- Push a 100-pound (45-kilogram) sandbag about 15 feet (4.5 meters) and return it to its original position.
- Climb a fence that is 6 feet (2 m) high.
- Drag a 160-pound (72-kg) dummy for 30 feet (9 m).
- Load and fire a weapon.
- Get through a narrow window.
- Walk across a beam that is 12 feet (3.6 m) in length.
- Run 500 feet (152 m) to the finish line.

SAMPLE QUESTIONS FROM A POLICE OFFICER EXAM

The following are examples of questions that applicants might find on a typical police officer written exam:

POLICE JUDGMENT QUIZZER

You have been assigned to a patrol post in the park during the winter months. You hear the cries of a boy who has fallen through the ice. The first thing you should do is:

   A. Rush to the nearest telephone and call an ambulance.
   B. Call upon a passerby to summon additional police officers.
   C. Rush to the spot from which the cries came and try to save the boy.
   D. Rush to the spot from which the cries came and question the boy concerning his identity so that you can summon his parents.

Answer: C

[Source: Fred M. Rafilson, *Master the Police Officer Exam*, 17th ed., 2005.]

OBSERVATION AND MEMORY

Study this photo for thirty seconds, and then answer the following questions:

- How many children are in the photograph?
- What do the children appear to be doing?
- What time of day is it?
- What color shirt is the man wearing?
- How many children are on the merry-go-round?

BASIC MATH

Officer Milton visits area businesses as part of a theft prevention program. If Officer Milton visits three area businesses every week, except for his three-week vacation, how many groups does he visit in one year?

A. 49
B. 98
C. 147
D. 150
E. 166

Answer: C

[Source: U.S. Capitol Police, *Study Guide and Sample Test for the National Police Officer Selection Test*, 2009.]

PSYCHOLOGICAL EVALUATION—
TYPICAL QUESTIONS:

- Why do you want to become a police officer?
- What are your strengths and weaknesses?
- What could make you lose your temper?
- What have you done in your past that you most regret?
- Are you afraid of dying?
- What is your attitude toward drugs?

[Source: Fred M. Rafilson, *Master the Police Officer Exam*, 17th ed., 2005]

Finally, candidates have to pass a medical exam. A doctor measures the person's blood pressure, height, weight, and heart function. Hearing, vision, and strength are also tested. The person may have to give blood and urine samples so that they can be tested for potential health problems, such as high cholesterol. A sample of the person's urine will probably be tested for traces of drugs. Any serious medical condition or evidence of illegal drug use can be enough reason for a candidate to be rejected. Even color blindness or being overweight can disqualify someone from joining the police force.

PERSONAL HISTORY, INTERVIEWS, AND BACKGROUND CHECKS

Knowing that a person can meet the physical and mental demands of the police force is not enough. An officer must also be honest and emotionally stable. To determine these qualities, the police department will first take a personal history. That personal history can be as long as thirty pages, and it might include questions such as the following:

- Where were you born?
- Where did you go to school?
- Where did you work?
- To what organizations did you belong?

The police department will confirm the information on these documents through a background investigation, criminal history check, and possibly a lie detector test. During the background check, an investigator may call the applicant's friends, relatives, neighbors, and coworkers and check public and private records to make sure that everything the person has said is true. The background investigation will include many important details of the applicant's life. Some of the information provided may be very personal or embarrassing, such as a history of the person's marriage, drug, and legal problems. During the lie detector test, the applicant is connected to a machine that can supposedly determine whether a statement is true or false. The machine measures any changes in heart rate, breathing rate, and blood pressure that might occur when someone is nervous.

The application process might also include several other tests. These tests can involve a written psychological evaluation and an interview with a psychologist to determine if the person is mentally stable enough to be a police officer. The candidate might also be asked to participate in an oral board interview.

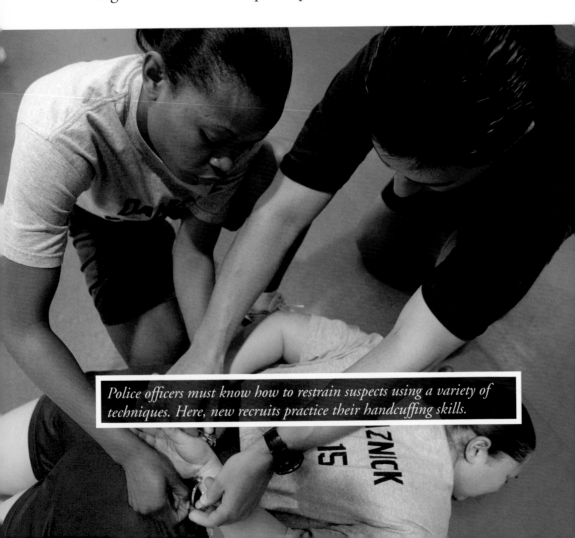

Police officers must know how to restrain suspects using a variety of techniques. Here, new recruits practice their handcuffing skills.

During this interview, a panel of commissioners, police personnel, or psychologists asks the person questions about different situations to determine if he or she has the knowledge, communication skills, integrity, and motivation needed to perform the job.

POLICE ACADEMY

Once someone is hired by a police force, he or she must go through training at a police academy. Many large local and state police forces have their own police academies. Smaller departments will send their recruits to train at a state or regional academy.

At the police academy, new recruits learn how to become successful police officers. Some recruits live at the academy while they train (this is especially true with federal law enforcement agencies). Other recruits commute from home daily. Trainees may remain at the academy for a few weeks or several months.

Officers must understand the laws and rules of the job by taking a variety of college-style classes on related subjects, including these:

- Arrest, search, and seizure procedures
- Use of firearms and deadly force
- Criminal and constitutional laws
- Civil rights
- State laws and local ordinances
- Writing citations (such as for traffic violations)
- Conducting interviews and interrogations
- Community relations
- Booking procedures for arrested suspects
- Handling evidence
- Writing reports

- Motor vehicle codes and traffic control
- Accident investigation
- Pursuit driving and other vehicle operations
- Use of warrants
- Police ethics and the Law Enforcement Code of Conduct
- Court procedures and testimony
- First-aid training
- Emergency response
- Crowd control
- Surveillance
- Defense tactics (such as handcuffing, self-defense, and search procedures)

Learning these skills in a classroom is important, but it's also vital for trainees to practice these skills for real so that they are prepared once they enter the police force. At the police academy, recruits may be placed in real-life situations in which they respond to a call as they would if they were actually working on the force.

To improve recruits' strength, endurance, and flexibility, the police academy also offers physical training courses that are as grueling as military basic training. "We had a 6:30 AM start time, and there were days we didn't leave until 7 at night," Kevin Murtagh recalls of his police academy days. "From the first day, we ran a mile and a half [2.4 kilometers], and we probably didn't run less than 4 to 5 miles [6 to 8 km] a day." Recruits also get toughened-up emotionally so that they can survive once they're out patrolling the streets. "If you can deal with the drill instructor literally an inch [2.54 centimeters] from your face screaming at you, it's mental toughness," says Murtagh. No matter how much instructors scream, recruits must always respond with a respectful "Yes, Sir!" or "Yes, Ma'am!"

The physical training classes at a police academy can be very demanding. Classes usually start by exercising as a group. Then each recruit performs many sets of push-ups, sit-ups, abdominal crunches, pull-ups, and a variety of other exercises. As part of self-defense training, recruits have to learn how to fight—and defend—themselves. This training may involve punching boxing bags, practicing street-fighting techniques (and weapon disarming), learning how to fall, and working with a police baton or Taser. Recruits may practice these techniques hundreds or even thousands of times before they get them right. They will also learn how to take apart firearms, clean them, and reassemble them. They practice shooting firearms over and over again in a variety of ways (such as while kneeling or lying on the ground) until using a weapon becomes second nature.

After graduating from a police academy, officers receive their police badge and certifications (in areas such as cardiopulmonary resuscitation [CPR], speed enforcement, or weapons), and a position with the police department to which they applied. Their training, however, does not end once they graduate from the police academy. For the first few months on the force, new officers are assigned to an experienced field training officer (FTO), who guides them and keeps track of their progress. The FTO evaluates the officers' performance for one year to eighteen months. Any new officers who do not meet the department's standards are let go. Those who make it through the probation period become officers.

MOVING UP THROUGH THE RANKS

Officers can become eligible for promotion after about three to five years. They may become a detective, specialize in a

Making it through the police academy can be a grueling, yet ultimately rewarding, experience. In this photograph, the New York Police Department's Police Academy graduates are sworn in as officers.

particular area of law enforcement (such as drug enforcement), or get promoted in rank to corporal, sergeant, lieutenant, and, finally, captain or chief of police. Whether an officer qualifies for a promotion is based on his or her written exam scores and job performance.

Officers can improve their performance by continuing their education at local colleges, police department academies, or federal agency training centers. The higher the rank of an officer, the more education is required for that position. For example, a sergeant may need only two years of college, whereas

a captain will likely have his or her four-year college degree. Getting additional training also helps officers keep on top of the latest law enforcement techniques and equipment. Some police departments will pay for their officers to complete their college education or obtain an advanced degree.

chapter 3

CAREERS IN LOCAL AND STATE LAW ENFORCEMENT

Police officers can work for local, state, or federal law enforcement departments. The educational requirements for local police departments are usually less strict than those for federal departments. To get a job with a city police department, a person may need only a high school diploma or general equivalency diploma, whereas a state patrol officer will usually need a college degree.

THE POLICE FORCE

Uniformed police officers can get hired with just a high school diploma and a year or two of related work experience (for example, working in security or the corrections system). Some police departments, however, require that candidates have completed a year or more of college. Many departments will pay all or part of college tuition. In Canada, most candidates have a diploma (degree) from a community college or regular college.

Officers work in police departments of different sizes, from small rural communities to big cities. Municipal (urban) police officers work within the city limits. County officers cover the areas outside cities. In small departments, officers may handle various jobs, from patrolling the streets to writing reports. Larger departments typically assign officers to a specific duty.

PATROL OFFICERS

Patrol officers are the public face of the police department. When someone calls 911 to report a burglary, murder, accident, or other emergency situation, patrol officers are sent to the scene. Patrol officers also drive through cities at night, looking for people who are acting suspiciously. If a crime is being committed, the officer may have to pursue and arrest suspects.

The life of a patrol officer isn't all about high-speed car chases and thrilling criminal cases. Officers may be called in to

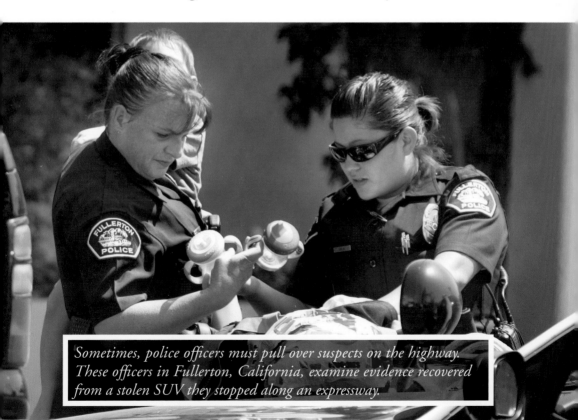

Sometimes, police officers must pull over suspects on the highway. These officers in Fullerton, California, examine evidence recovered from a stolen SUV they stopped along an expressway.

assist with all kinds of situations, from settling a dispute between a husband and wife, to getting a cat out of a tree.

Patrol officers must be good problem solvers, able to think on their feet no matter how unexpected the situation might be. They must have a good understanding of local laws and ordinances so that they know how to respond to various incidents. Moreover, patrol officers can never lose their cool. They must always remain calm under pressure.

A detective in Little Rock, Arkansas, investigates an abandoned building. He is looking for a suspect who is wanted in a drug investigation.

TRAFFIC OFFICERS

Traffic officers are uniformed officers who patrol the roads and highways of every town, city, and state, enforcing traffic laws. Traffic officers may be found parked by the side of a highway using a radar gun to catch speeders. Once they catch someone, they will check the person's license and registration and issue a ticket. Traffic officers also perform routine vehicle checks, looking for drivers who have been drinking or taking illegal drugs, or who may have committed a crime. Sometimes a traffic officer will have to arrest a driver who is breaking the law.

Traffic officers also may be found at the scene of an accident. They will help people who were injured in the crash, call for an ambulance, and direct traffic around the accident. Officers often investigate the cause of accidents, and they may have to report what they find in court. Sometimes traffic officers spend their days monitoring parking meters and issuing tickets to cars that are parked at expired meters.

Traffic officers need only a high school diploma or its equivalent. In addition, they must have a year of experience working in a public agency or security job, or serving in the U.S. military. Because they spend a lot of time in a patrol car, traffic officers definitely need to have a valid driver's license.

DETECTIVES

Detectives usually do not wear a uniform. Sometimes detectives specialize in one law enforcement area, such as arson, burglary, murder, drugs, organized crime, forgery, gang activity, identity theft, computer forensics, gambling, or financial crimes. Other detectives can be assigned to just about any type of crime.

PROFILE OF AN INVESTIGATIVE AGENT

When local police departments are unable to solve a crime on their own, they call in their state investigative agency. For police departments in Georgia, that agency is the Georgia Bureau of Investigation (GBI). Jesse Maddox has been with the GBI for twelve years. Today, he is the Assistant Special Agent in Charge at the organization.

Like many investigative agents, Maddox started his career as a police officer. To get a job with the GBI, he had to take a state merit exam that tested his memory, observation, and problem-solving skills. He also had to take a lie detector test and undergo a background check. Finally, he went through several weeks of special training, in addition to his police training, for the GBI.

Maddox and other GBI agents help local police or sheriff's offices with criminal investigations, such as violent crimes or thefts involving large amounts of money (hundreds of thousands of dollars or more). GBI agents conduct interviews and gather evidence to try to determine what happened during the crime. "Once we've gathered the evidence to make an arrest, we present that case to the district attorney," Maddox says.

When a crime is committed, a uniformed police officer is usually the first person on the scene. The officer questions witnesses, gathers whatever evidence he or she can find, and arrests any suspects. If the crime remains unsolved, one or more detectives are assigned to the case.

Detectives are problem solvers. They investigate crime scenes, looking for the tiniest details to help them determine when the crime occurred, where it occurred, what happened, and what the criminal's motive might have been. To answer these questions, detectives have to search the scene and gather evidence, such as fingerprints, photographs, bullet fragments, hair, and skin. These pieces of evidence are sent to a crime laboratory. At the lab, technicians use computers to match the evidence with fingerprints and other information from known criminals. During the investigation, detectives also interview people on and around the scene of the crime, including uniformed police officers, victims, witnesses, and possible suspects. Sometimes detectives will use legal surveillance techniques, listening in on suspects' phone conversations or following them around to monitor their activities.

After the detective has collected all possible evidence in a case, he or she will write a report of the crime and submit it to a superior officer. Based on the available evidence, that officer may decide to arrest a suspect (or suspects). The evidence may be used in court during the criminal trial.

Police departments and private companies both hire detectives. Although a college degree is not required, some police departments expect their detectives to have at least a year or two of college. Classes in criminal justice, law, and foreign languages all can be assets in this field. Many detectives start out as police officers. After working as a uniformed officer for several months to a few years and passing a series of tests, candidates may be considered for the position of detective.

K-9 OFFICERS AND MOUNTED POLICE

K-9 and mounted police officers have many of the same responsibilities as other uniformed officers. Instead of having another officer as a partner, though, they have a dog or horse. K-9 officers work with dogs that are specially trained to sniff out bombs or drugs, search for people who are lost or who have committed a crime, and control crowds. Many large city police departments have their own K-9 units.

K-9 officers may be found in many different working situations and surroundings, including airports, seaports, and U.S. borders. At the airport, they may search incoming luggage for illegal substances. At the borders between the United States and Mexico and the United States and Canada, a trained K-9 team can catch people who are trying to enter the country illegally. At the scene of a building collapse, a K-9 team may be called in to help find victims who are buried underneath the rubble.

In a K-9 unit, both the dog and the officer (called a handler) require special training. The officer learns how to work as a team with his or her canine partner, as well as how to care for the dog. The dog learns skills such as obedience, pursuit, and how to track a scent.

In mounted police units, it is common for police officers and their horses to be involved in crowd control because it's much easier to pass through a crowd on a horse

than in a police car. In Canada, the Royal Mounted Police serve as that country's police force. They have been in existence since 1873, and they're recognized by their distinctive red uniforms and ranger hats.

K-9 dogs help their human partners look for evidence and catch criminals. This K-9 dog is learning how to take down a suspect.

Becoming a mounted police officer requires a lot of training and a commitment to hard work. Trainees are usually seasoned police officers. Training can last from fourteen to twenty weeks, depending on the police department. Mounted police officers not only have to learn how to ride their horses extremely well— often in crowded situations—but also have to feed and care for their horses and even clean their stalls.

SHERIFFS

Sheriffs perform jobs similar to those of uniformed local or county police chiefs. They are in charge of enforcing the laws in their county. Most sheriffs' departments are small, with fewer than twenty-five officers.

Sheriffs conduct criminal investigations. They also arrest people who are breaking the law and process them through the court system and county jail. Sheriffs perform other general law enforcement tasks. A sheriff is often the highest law enforcement position in a county and is usually elected to the position. The sheriff's department may have deputy sheriffs to help transport prisoners or provide security in courtrooms. Requirements for this job are similar to those for a police officer. Applicants usually have to be at least twenty-one years old, a U.S. citizen, and have a high school diploma or its equivalent, and they must go through the police academy or a similar training program.

STATE POLICE

State police officers, sometimes also called state troopers, carry out many of the same functions as local police officers do. But they work for their state, rather than for a city or county within the state. Depending on the state, some of the jobs that state police officers may perform include making arrests, investigating crimes, providing emergency assistance at the scene of a traffic accident, patrolling state highways, and searching people or property for illegal or stolen goods.

To become a state police officer, an applicant must have a college degree. He or she then must complete training at the state police academy.

OTHER JOBS IN LAW ENFORCEMENT

The jobs described in this chapter aren't the only positions available in law enforcement. Many opportunities in this field fall under different categories, including the following jobs:

- Crime prevention officer, who teaches crime prevention methods to businesses and schools
- Fugitive search officer, who finds and brings to justice people who have committed a crime and have run from the law
- Fish and game warden, who makes sure that hunters and fishermen are following the law
- Harbor patrol officer, who rescues ships and people who are in danger or distress, and finds and arrests criminals who use the waterways
- Hostage negotiation officer, who rescues people who are being held hostage
- Juvenile officer, who protects children who are the victims of abuse or neglect, finds lost or runaway children, and takes into custody children who commit crimes
- Special Weapons and Tactics (SWAT) officer, who assists police officers during emergency situations, such as riots or hostage standoffs

SWAT teams are often called in to assist with dangerous situations. Here, a U.S. Capitol Police SWAT team storms a government building on Capitol Hill after people tried to get through a checkpoint with what looked like a gun.

- Vice officer, who finds and arrests people who are involved in illegal activities with drugs, liquor, gambling, or obscenity
- Transit authority officer, who patrols subways, buses, and other public transportation services
- Bomb squad officer, who responds to bomb threats and uses robots and trained dogs to find and disarm explosives

People who enjoy law enforcement, but who don't want to become uniformed officers, should not give up on this career. Every police department needs a variety of people to support the work of its uniformed officers. Employees working in recruitment, accounting, employee services, public relations, data collecting and reporting, transportation, and the crime laboratory are crucial to the efforts of the police department.

chapter 4

CAREERS IN FEDERAL LAW ENFORCEMENT

Applicants for any job in federal law enforcement will usually need to have a bachelor's degree and at least three years of related work experience. Once they are hired, they will go through several weeks of specialized training with their agency. Most federal agents are trained at either the U.S. Marine Corps base in Quantico, Virginia, or the Federal Law Enforcement Training Center in Glynco, Georgia.

FEDERAL BUREAU OF INVESTIGATION

The Federal Bureau of Investigation (FBI) is the government's main investigative department. An FBI agent's job is to protect the country from terrorist attacks, cyber (computer) attacks, organized crime, and violent crimes. Some of the crimes the FBI may look into include money laundering, kidnapping, drug trafficking, bank robbery, terrorism, foreign spying, and civil rights abuses.

The FBI has been in existence for more than one hundred years. The organization is based in Washington, D.C., but it has fifty-six field offices in big cities across the United States, about four hundred agencies in smaller U.S. cities, and more than sixty offices around the world.

Working for the FBI can be very exciting. One week an agent may be interviewing sources to gather evidence for a terrorism case, and the next week he or she may be trailing a suspected Mafia boss. However, it is more difficult to land a job with the FBI than with a local police force. Applicants must hold a college degree and have at least three years of professional work experience. Or they must have an advanced college degree, such as a master's degree, and two years of professional work experience. It is helpful for agents to have majored in an area such as computer science, information technology, a foreign language, or law.

Before being considered for a job with the FBI, applicants must go through a very thorough background check to make sure they do not have a criminal past. After getting hired, all FBI agents complete eighteen weeks of training

Suspects often leave evidence, including fingerprints, at the scene of a crime. In high-profile crimes, the Federal Bureau of Investigation (FBI) may be called in to help collect evidence.

at the FBI Academy on the U.S. Marine Corps base in Quantico, Virginia.

DRUG ENFORCEMENT

U.S. Drug Enforcement Administration (DEA) agents oversee and enforce federal laws that relate to controlled and illegal substances, particularly those involving narcotics and other unsafe drugs. They arrest and prosecute people who grow, make, sell, or distribute illegal drugs, or who are involved in violence related to drugs. DEA agents may go undercover or travel to other countries to monitor and shut down illegal drug organizations.

DEA agents must be at least twenty-one years old but no older than thirty-six. They should be a U.S. citizen and hold a college degree. (Special consideration is given to those who hold degrees in criminal justice or police science.) They need to have graduated with at least a 2.95 grade point average (about a B minus). Otherwise, they may have one year of experience conducting criminal investigations, three years of work experience plus special skills (such as those required for a pilot, accountant, or linguist), or a law degree. The application process can take up to a year. It includes a qualifications review, written test, panel interview, medical exam, physical test, lie detector test, psychological test, and background investigation. A drug test is one of the most important parts of the application process. For obvious reasons, the DEA does not want to hire special agents who are using illegal drugs.

Once hired, new DEA agents must go through fourteen weeks of training at the DEA Training Academy on the Marine Corps base at Quantico, Virginia. There, they learn skills such as defense tactics, intelligence gathering, and use of firearms.

LAW ENFORCEMENT AFTER THE TERRORIST ATTACKS OF 9/11

On September 11, 2001, Al Qaeda terrorists launched the worst case of terrorism in U.S. history when they hijacked planes and crashed two of them into the twin towers in New York City and a third into the Pentagon just outside Washington, D.C. These attacks forced the U.S. government and law enforcement agencies to change tactics and focus their efforts on a new kind of threat on American soil.

The 9/11 terrorist attacks led to improved teamwork between federal and state law enforcement agencies. Even small, community police officers began learning how to identify possible terrorist threats and report them to the FBI or other intelligence agencies. Police departments around the country also learned how to respond quickly and efficiently in the event of another terrorist attack.

THE BUREAU OF ALCOHOL, TOBACCO, FIREARMS, AND EXPLOSIVES

The Bureau of Alcohol, Tobacco, Firearms, and Explosives (ATF) is a law enforcement agency within the U.S. Department of Justice that protects the public from violent crimes. Its agents investigate crimes related to firearms, explosives, alcohol, and tobacco. An ATF agent may perform surveillance, conduct raids of suspects' homes or businesses, and prepare evidence to present in court.

To get a job with the ATF, applicants must be at least twenty-one years old and hold a college degree. Once they are hired, they must go through training at the Federal Law Enforcement Training Center in Glynco, Georgia. There, they learn about surveillance, arrest techniques, firearms use, and explosives investigation.

DEPARTMENT OF HOMELAND SECURITY

After the September 11, 2001, terrorist attacks on the World Trade Center in New York City and the Pentagon outside Washington, D.C., officials of the U.S. government knew the nation needed a new kind of security force. The U.S. Department of Homeland Security (DHS) was established by Congress and the president in 2002 to prevent terrorist attacks and aid in recovery efforts should another attack occur. Protecting the country from terrorism involves patrolling public transit systems, landmarks, ports, and power plants; increasing security at major events, such as Fourth of July celebrations; and securing the nation's borders to prevent terrorists from sneaking into the United States.

The U.S. Customs and Border Protection, a division within the DHS, includes uniformed men and women who make up the biggest law enforcement group in the country. Border Patrol agents, for example, must be U.S. citizens, and they should be under the age of thirty-seven when they are

U.S. Border Patrol agents are part of the Department of Homeland Security. Here, a Border Patrol vehicle looks for signs of illegal activity along the U.S.-Mexico border.

hired. They must have a bachelor's degree or previous related experience (for example, as a police officer), and pass an exam that evaluates their language and reasoning skills.

A number of different jobs are available within the DHS besides Border Patrol agent, including U.S. Immigration and Customs Enforcement Special Agent, U.S. Secret Service agent, and U.S. Coast Guard Officer.

Each of these agencies within the DHS has its own job requirements. People who are interested in a career with the DHS can check directly with the organization for individual job descriptions. (See the "For More Information" section at the back of this book.)

U.S. SECRET SERVICE

The U.S. Secret Service was created in the 1800s. Back then, its job was to prevent criminals from producing and using counterfeit money. The agency still has these duties. It also safeguards the country's financial and payment system. Its main responsibility today, however, is to protect national leaders, including the U.S. president, visiting heads of state, the U.S. vice president, and their families. Secret Service agents are the men and women who, if necessary, will place their own body in the path of an assassin's bullet to save the president's life.

To become a Secret Service agent, a person must be between twenty-one and thirty-seven years old. He or she must have graduated from college in the top third of the class or have one year of experience working in a law enforcement or investigative position. The application process involves a physical fitness evaluation, written test, and interviews. Because the job involves protecting the most important position in the country—the president—applicants must get top-secret clearance by passing a lie detector test, drug screening, and a thorough background check.

U.S. Secret Service agents must keep a careful watch over the president of the United States. They may even have to throw themselves in the line of fire to protect the commander in chief.

FEDERAL AIR MARSHAL SERVICE

Federal air marshals in the Federal Air Marshal Service work for the Transportation Security Administration (TSA), which is part of the DHS. Their job is to protect the security of airline passengers. The United States first started its sky marshal program in 1970, following the hijacking of several commercial airplanes. But after terrorists flew planes into the towers of the World Trade Center and Pentagon on September 11, 2001, security in the air became a top priority and the program was expanded.

Federal air marshals work in airports and fly on selected commercial flights. They don't wear uniforms because they must look like the other passengers. If trouble occurs on a flight, they use their specialized training in firearms and self-defense to

Federal air marshals must be ready to respond to any threat in the air. Hijacking simulations like this one help prepare new air marshals for their job.

keep the passengers safe. Federal air marshals must be U.S. citizens, younger than thirty-seven at the time of appointment, and have three years of experience in law enforcement, security, or another professional field.

U.S. MARSHALS SERVICE

The U.S. Marshals Service is the oldest law enforcement agency in the United States. It has been in existence since 1789, and it still plays a very important role in the criminal justice system. The program includes ninety-four U.S. Marshals (one for each federal court district), and more than three thousand Deputy U.S. Marshals and criminal investigators. Deputy U.S. Marshals have all the following responsibilities:

- Bringing in fugitives who are wanted for federal crimes
- Protecting judges and jurors during federal court cases
- Running the Witness Security Program, which protects people whose lives may be in jeopardy after they testify against dangerous criminals
- Transporting federal prisoners
- Retrieving property that has been acquired by criminals through illegal activities

Requirements for U.S. Marshals are similar to those of other federal law enforcement positions. Applicants must be between the ages of twenty-one and thirty-six. They must have a four-year college degree, three years of related work experience, or a combination of education and work experience. After being hired, recruits have to complete a seventeen-week basic-training program in Glynco, Georgia.

chapter 5

THE BENEFITS, RISKS, AND FUTURE OUTLOOK OF THE CAREER

Working as a police officer can be very fun and rewarding. One of the biggest advantages is the excitement that comes with the job. For those who crave adventure, this is an ideal career.

"After twenty-seven-plus years, I still enjoy my job," says Robin Matthews, an inspector (detective) with the San Francisco Police Department. "I grew up wanting to be a police officer since I was a young child, and it didn't disappoint me. It never got boring, and every day was different."

Working in a job that involves saving lives can be especially satisfying. A lot of respect and pride comes from wearing a police officer's uniform. "At the end of the day, I'm thankful and very proud of my profession," says Jennifer McFeggan, of the Hamilton Police Service in Ontario, Canada.

The field of law enforcement also involves many challenges. Being a police officer in real life is far different from how it is portrayed on television. Police officers are not always involved in thrilling car chases or shootouts. Much of the time, officers sit at their desks and fill out paperwork or patrol quiet streets. They may have to work long hours or stay outside in cold or stormy weather.

Often, even an officer's best efforts cannot bring criminals to justice. It can be frustrating for an officer to learn that he or she worked hard to arrest a suspect, only to be told that the court system released that person without requiring him or her to serve any jail time.

One of the most difficult issues for officers to deal with is the loss of life that can occur on their watch. For GBI agents like Jesse Maddox, knowing that someone he was trying to protect has died is really difficult, especially when the crime involves a child. "It just plays over and over in your head," he says. "You can't stay totally emotionless because you wouldn't have any passion for your job, but you do need to stay detached."

HOURS AND BENEFITS

Although law enforcement isn't a traditional nine-to-five job (it's common to work nights, weekends, and holidays—especially for

Being a police officer is not just about car chases and hunting down criminals. It involves a lot of paperwork, and officers often find themselves spending long hours behind a desk.

junior officers), the hours are reasonable. Most police officers and detectives work at least a forty-hour week. Sometimes when they are working on a particularly difficult investigation, officers and detectives will have to work overtime. In those situations,

Thanks to technology, police officers can keep watch without having to leave their station. This New Jersey police officer monitors a remote surveillance camera.

officers will receive extra pay (usually their full hourly pay rate, plus half of that rate).

Police officers get excellent benefits, which include paid vacation, sick leave, health and life insurance, and sometimes college tuition assistance. People in most professions have to wait until they are sixty-five or seventy years old to retire and receive their pension. Police officers, however, can retire with their full benefits after just twenty-five years of service. Depending on when they started working for their police department, some officers are young enough when they retire to start a new career.

OPPORTUNITIES AND EARNINGS

According to the U.S. Department of Labor's Bureau of Labor Statistics, demand is increasing for law enforcement due to the continuing threat of terrorism and drug-related crimes. As a result, employment opportunities for police officers are expected to rise faster than open jobs in other occupations.

Opportunities in most local police departments are excellent. Ordinarily, these departments have

THE DANGERS OF BEING A POLICE OFFICER

Anyone who listens to the evening news will have likely heard some report about police officers getting killed or injured in the line of duty. Law enforcement can be a very dangerous career. People who commit crimes are willing to break the law—and that includes using a weapon and deadly force against an officer. An average 164 officers are killed in the line of duty each year, according to the National Law Enforcement Officers Memorial Fund. This constant threat can be stressful both to officers and their families.

People who enter this profession must do so with the understanding that they may have to put their lives at risk. "It's a risk you accept. You certainly know it's there," says South Plainfield, New Jersey, police lieutenant Kevin Murtagh. "You train, and you do as you were trained. And if you train hard and you train well, you pray to God that your training kicks in and you go home at the end of the tour."

plenty of open positions that need to be filled. Qualified applicants have a good chance of getting hired. Competition for open jobs at state and federal agencies is much tougher because the salaries are generally higher. As a result, the demand for jobs in state and federal departments is greater than the number of jobs available, and these departments can be very selective about which candidates they hire. Applicants can give themselves an advantage in the hiring process by getting a college degree and/or experience in the military or police science. In Canada, the job market is somewhat tighter than in the United States. The number of applicants is about equal to the number of job openings.

Earnings vary based on the position and type of department. People with a college degree will typically earn more than those who have only a high school education. (For specific police officer salary information, see the *Occupational Outlook Handbook, 2008–2009*, on the Bureau of Labor Statistics Web site, http://www.bls.gov/oco/ocos160.htm.)

Law enforcement provides plenty of room for advancement for talented, hard-working officers. When an officer is hired, there is usually a probation period of six months to three years. After officers prove themselves, they become eligible for a promotion. Some officers move up to detective or begin specializing in one area, such as juvenile law enforcement.

THE FUTURE JOB OUTLOOK IN LAW ENFORCEMENT

No job is completely recession-proof—even a job in law enforcement. The number of police jobs is based on how much money local, state, and federal governments have available to spend on their police forces. That amount can vary from year to year. If government budgets get trimmed, law enforcement jobs can be cut as well.

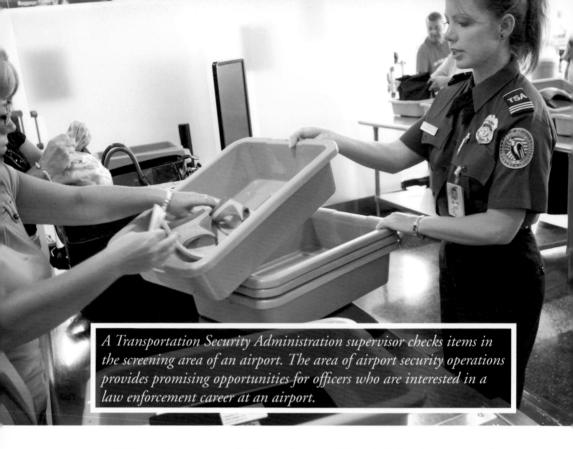

A Transportation Security Administration supervisor checks items in the screening area of an airport. The area of airport security operations provides promising opportunities for officers who are interested in a law enforcement career at an airport.

When the state of Georgia was hit with budget cuts during a recession, the GBI felt the pinch. "Not only are we losing money, we lose positions, we lose people, and we lose vehicles," explains Maddox. "We actually closed two work units this year—the identity theft unit and the state drug task force. So it's far from recession-proof." Murtagh says his department in New Jersey was told to trim 10 percent off their budget in 2008 and 2009. They have even started to talk about laying off members of his police department.

Overall, though, law enforcement remains an exciting, meaningful, and profitable profession. For people who pursue a career as a police officer or one of the many other jobs available in the field, there are still plenty of opportunities. Police officers enjoy good salaries, excellent benefits, and the satisfaction that comes from saving lives and making a real difference in their communities.

glossary

academic Educational; relating to instructional studies or an educational institution.

assault A physical attack on another person or people.

beat An area that is assigned to a police officer to patrol.

cardiopulmonary resuscitation (CPR) An emergency life-saving method that uses breathing and chest compressions to keep a sick or injured person alive until medical help arrives.

citation A penalty for a minor offense, such as a traffic violation.

constable An officer who serves court papers and transports prisoners.

controlled substances Any drug as defined in the five categories of the Controlled Substances Act of 1970.

conviction The act of finding someone guilty of a crime, or an instance of being found guilty.

corrections system The treatment of convicted offenders through a process of imprisonment, rehabilitation, probation, and parole.

counterfeit Made as a copy of something, such as money, in order to deceive people.

deoxyribonucleic acid (DNA) The genetic material inside every cell that determines a person's characteristics.

dishonorable discharge Dismissal from the armed forces as punishment for wrongdoing.

entry-level Being at the lowest level of an employment hierarchy.

ethics A system of moral principles that governs the appropriate conduct of a person or group.

felony A serious crime, such as murder.

forensic Scientific techniques, such as DNA analysis, that are used to investigate a crime.

fugitive A person who has committed a crime and is running from the police or other law enforcement officials.

integrity The quality of being honest and having good character.

interrogation A method of questioning that the police can use when investigating a suspect.

Mafia A criminal organization in the United States that originated in Sicily, Italy. It usually is involved in international drug dealing, racketeering, and gambling, among other activities.

money laundering To hide the origin of illegally gained money so that it appears to be legal.

motive A person's reason for committing a crime (for example, revenge).

narcotics Drugs, which may be obtained legally with a doctor's prescription, or illegally.

obscenity Something that is considered offensive based on a society's standards of morality.

ordinance A rule or law made by a local government.

pension A regular payment provided by an employer that a person receives after he or she retires.

probation A period of time in which a person has to prove himself or herself on the job.

prosecute To take legal action against someone; to have someone tried in a court of law for a civil or criminal offense.

surveillance Closely watching or following a person or people who are suspected of having committed a crime.

Taser A weapon used by the police that sends out a current of electricity to momentarily stun a suspect.

warden The official who is in charge of a prison or jail.

warrant A document giving police specific rights or powers, such as the right to search or arrest someone.

for more information

Bureau of Alcohol, Tobacco, Firearms, and Explosives
650 Massachusetts Avenue, Room 8400
Washington, DC 20226
(202) 927-8480
Web site: http://www.atf.gov
This federal agency enforces federal criminal laws and regulates
the explosives and firearms industries.

Bureau of Labor Statistics
U.S. Department of Labor
2 Massachusetts Avenue NE, Suite 2135
Washington, DC 20212-0001
(202) 691-5700
Web site: http://www.bls.gov
The BLS annually updates the *Occupational Outlook
Handbook*, which describes thousands of careers and
provides details about requirements and salaries.

Canadian Police Association
141 Catherine Street, Suite 100
Ottawa, ON K2P 1C3
Canada
(613) 231-4168
Web site: http://www.cpa-acp.ca
The Canadian Police Association represents the interests
of the more than fifty thousand police officers and personnel across Canada.

Department of Homeland Security
U.S. Department of Homeland Security

Washington, DC 20528
(202) 282-8000
Web site: http://www.dhs.gov
The Department of Homeland Security secures the
    nation from the numerous threats it faces daily. For
    career-related information, see http://www.dhs.gov/
    xabout/careers.

Federal Bureau of Investigation (FBI)
J. Edgar Hoover Building
935 Pennsylvania Avenue NW
Washington, DC 20535-0001
(202) 324-3000
Web site: http://www.fbi.gov
The FBI is the principal investigative arm of the U.S.
    Department of Justice. Besides investigating specific
    crimes, it assists state and local law enforcement agencies.

National Association of Police Officers (NAPO)
750 First Street NE, Suite 920
Washington, DC 20002
(202) 842-4420
Web site: http://www.napo.org
The NAPO works to improve working conditions for the
    country's law enforcement officers.

National Law Enforcement Recruiters Association
2045 Fifteenth Street North, Suite 210
Arlington, VA 22201
(703)528-5600
Web site: http://www.nlera.org
This organization helps recruit qualified candidates into law
    enforcement positions throughout the country.

Police Employment
Web site: http://www.policeemployment.com
This online job information center provides career information
and requirements for various law enforcement positions.

Royal Canadian Mounted Police
RCMP Public Affairs and Communications Services
Headquarters Building
1200 Vanier Parkway
Ottawa, ON K1A 0R2
Canada
(613) 993-7267
Web site: http://www.rcmp-grc.gc.ca
The Royal Canadian Mounted Police, or Mounties, is
Canada's national police service.

USAJOBS
(703) 724-1850
Web site: http://www.usajobs.gov
This is the official job site of the federal government.

WEB SITES

Due to the changing nature of Internet links, Rosen Publishing
has developed an online list of Web sites related to the subject
of this book. This site is updated regularly. Please use this link
to access the list:

http://www.rosenlinks.com/ecar/poli

for further reading

Ackerman, Thomas H. *FBI Careers: The Ultimate Guide to Landing a Job as One of America's Finest.* 2nd ed. Indianapolis, IN: JIST Works, 2005.

Ackerman, Thomas H. *Federal Law Enforcement Careers: Profiles of 250 High-Powered Positions and Tactics for Getting Hired.* 2nd ed. Indianapolis, IN: JIST Works, 2006.

Baker, Barry M. *Becoming a Police Officer: An Insider's Guide to a Career in Law Enforcement.* Lincoln, NE: iUniverse, 2006.

De Capua, Sarah. *The FBI* (Cornerstones of Freedom). New York, NY: Children's Press, 2007.

Ferguson. *Law Enforcement* (Discovering Careers for Your Future). New York, NY: Ferguson Publishing Company, 2008.

Fridell, Ron. *Forensic Science* (Cool Science). Minneapolis, MN: Lerner Publishing, 2007.

Harr, J. Scott, and Karen M. Hess. *Careers in Criminal Justice and Related Fields: From Internship to Promotion.* 5th ed. Belmont, CA: Wadsworth Publishing, 2006.

Lane, Brian, and Laura Buller. *Crime and Detection* (DK Eyewitness Books). New York, NY: DK Publishing, Inc., 2005.

Meyer, Jared. *Homeland Security Officers* (Extreme Careers). New York, NY: Rosen Publishing Group, 2007.

Palmiotto, Michael J., and Alison McKenney Brown. *McGraw-Hill's Police Officer Exams.* New York, NY: McGraw-Hill, 2008.

Reeves, Diane Lindsey, and Don Rauf. *Career Ideas for Teens in Government and Public Service.* New York, NY: Facts On File, 2005.

Reeves, Diane Lindsey, and Gail Karlitz. *Career Ideas for Teens in Law and Public Safety.* New York, NY: Checkmark Books, 2006.

Schroeder, Donald J. *Barron's Police Officer Exams.* 8th ed. Hauppauge, NY: Barron's, 2009.

Thomas, Wiliam David. *Working in Law Enforcement* (My Future Career). Milwaukee, WI: Gareth Stevens Publishing, 2005.

Townsend, John. *Lawmakers and the Police* (Painful History of Crime). Mankato, MN: Heinemann-Raintree Publishers, 2005.

bibliography

Baxter, Neale J. *Opportunities in Government Careers*. New York, NY: McGraw-Hill, 2001.

California Commission on Peace Officer Standards and Training. "How Do I Become a Peace Officer?" Retrieved May 7, 2009 (http://www.post.ca.gov/faqs/become.asp).

Colvin, Ross. "U.S. Recession Fuels Crime Rise, Police Chiefs Say." Reuters, January 27, 2009. Retrieved July 30, 2009 (http://www.reuters.com/article/domesticNews/idUSTRE50Q6FR20090127).

Goldberg, Jan. *Careers for Courageous People and Other Adventurous Types*. New York, NY: McGraw-Hill, 2005.

Interview with Jennifer McFeggan, Senior Constable, Hamilton Police Service. July 14, 2009.

Interview with Jesse Maddox, Assistant Special Agent in Charge, Georgia Bureau of Investigation. July 13, 2009.

Interview with Kevin Murtagh, Lieutenant, South Plainfield Police Department, New Jersey. July 13, 2009.

Interview with Robin Matthews, Inspector, San Francisco Police Department, California. July 6, 2009.

Jist Publishing. *America's Top 300 Jobs: A Complete Career Handbook*. 9th ed. Indianapolis, IN: JIST Publishing, Inc., 2004.

Learning Express. *Police Officer Exam*. New York, NY: LearningExpress LLC, 1999.

National Law Enforcement Officers Memorial Fund. "Law Enforcement Officers Killed in the Line of Duty/Past Ten Years (1999–2008)." March 2008. Retrieved August 20, 2009 (http://www.nleomf.com/TheMemorial/Facts/killedlod.htm).

Piddock, Charles. "Behind the Badge: Crime Fighting as a Career." *Career World*, September 2004, Volume 33, Issue 1, pp. 18–21.

Rafilson, Fred M. *Master the Police Officer Exam.* 17th ed. Lawrenceville, NJ: Thomson Peterson's, 2005.

Scholastic Action. "Undercover: A Career as a Cop." December 11, 2000, Volume 24, Issue 6, pp. 20–21.

U.S. Bureau of Labor Statistics. "Police and Detectives." *Occupational Outlook Handbook, 2008–2009 Edition.* Retrieved May 11, 2009 (http://www.bls.gov/oco/ocos160.htm).

U.S. Capitol Police. "Study Guide and Sample Test for the National Police Officer Selection Test." Retrieved August 21, 2009 (http://www.uscapitolpolice.gov/post_study_guide_09.pdf).

index

ABOUT THE AUTHOR

Stephanie Watson is a writer and editor based in Atlanta, Georgia. She has written or contributed to more than two dozen books, including *Anderson Cooper: Profile of a TV Journalist* and *How to Break in as a Television Producer*. She is a regular contributor of career reports to the Institute for Career Research, which provides vocational guidance information for young adults.

PHOTO CREDITS

Cover, p. 1 (background) © www.istockphoto.com/Jodie Coston; cover, p. 1 (inset) © www.istockphoto.com/Karen Mower; p. 4 Paul J. Richards/AFP/Getty Images; p. 6 © www.istockphoto.com/Marco Maccarini; pp. 10–11, 12–13, 31, 46–47 Shutterstock.com; pp. 14–15 Justin Sullivan/ Getty Images; pp. 16–17 Darren McCollester/Getty Images; pp. 18–19 Mike Simons/AFP/Getty Images; pp. 20–21, 34 Mario Tama/Getty Images; pp. 25, 28, 42, 63, 68 © AP Images; p. 26 Spencer Platt/Getty Images; pp. 38–39 Stephen Chernin/Getty Images; p. 41 © Bruce Chambers/The Orange County Register/Zuma Press; p. 50 Tim Sloan/Getty Images; p. 53 FBI; pp. 56–57 David McNew/Getty Images; p. 59 Saul Loeb/AFP/Getty Images; p. 60 Tom Mihalek/AFP/Getty Images; pp. 64–65 Jeff Zelevansky/Getty Images; p. 66 © www.istockphoto.com/Lisa Marzano.

Designer: Matt Cauli; Editor: Kathy Kuhtz Campbell; Photo Researcher: Amy Feinberg

JAN - - 2011

Northport-East Northport Public Library

To view your patron record from a computer, click on the Library's homepage: **www.nenpl.org**

You may:
- request an item be placed on hold
- renew an item that is overdue
- view titles and due dates checked out on your card
- view your own outstanding fines

151 Laurel Avenue
Northport, NY 11768
631-261-6930